AMELIA SAINT GEORGE'S

BEDROOM
AND BATHROOM
STENCIL KIT

INCLUDES 8 PULL-OUT STENCILS

EBURY PRESS

LONDON

TO MY GOD DAUGHTER
Maÿlis

First published in 1997

1 3 5 7 9 10 8 6 4 2

Text copyright © Amelia Saint George 1997
Photography copyright © Ebury Press 1997

First published in the United Kingdom in 1997 by Ebury Press,
Random House, 20 Vauxhall Bridge Road, London SW1V 2SA

Random House Australia (Pty) Limited, 20 Alfred Street, Milsons Point,
Sydney, New South Wales 2061, Australia

Random House New Zealand Limited, 18 Poland Road, Glenfield,
Auckland 10, New Zealand

Random House South Africa (Pty) Limited
Endulini, 5a Jubilee Road, Parktown 2193, South Africa

Random House UK Limited Reg. No. 954009

A catalogue record for this book is available from the British Library.

ISBN 0 09 182821 X

Editor Emma Callery
Designer Paul Wood
Photographer John Freeman

Printed and bound in Hong Kong by Sheck Wah Tong

C o n t e n t s

Introduction

Over the many years that I have been stencilling, I have discovered that the most successful bedrooms I have decorated have been stencilled simply, and yet creatively. A floral border on the wall with leaves scattered beneath works strikingly well, as does a single pillow covered with flowers while the next has but a single leaf. Equally, clusters of olives stencilled as a soothing frieze combined with small sprigs tumbling over curtains and voile netting, or perhaps just as soft traces over the window panes, quickly add depth to a bedroom. Or for a nursery, consider stencilling an array of hearts onto a baby's quilt, neatly align them over simple white tiles, and scatter the same hearts over a changing mat. Such diversity demonstrates the versatility of stencilling.

The beauty of stencils is that they can be developed to suit any style of decor. So if you are looking for a softly feminine room, think of stencilling muted flowers over silk curtains; but for the more dramatic among you, perhaps black geometric motifs stencilled onto cushions and bed linen are the perfect addition to a minimalist setting.

The bathroom is a more functional room. Whether luxurious or basic, it should be easy to clean; and this should be applied to changing mat, basin or large Jacuzzi set in marble surround. Fortunately, as stencilling is adaptable, easy, versatile and individual, it is perfect for any bathroom. Whatever your taste, there is a stencil in this book that will fit your bathroom. Ranging from a leafy twist to a wrought-iron motif via a perky boat for the nursery, you will find just what you are looking for here.

The *Bedroom and Bathroom Stencil Kit* is informative and practical, demonstrating how to use stencils on all manner of surfaces, such as fabric, sisal matting, glass, wood, lamps, walls, and tiles. Furthermore, within this book there are eight pages of stencils – each of which is described in great detail in its relevant chapter. The stencils are printed on special paper so that they are ready to cut out and use. All you need to do is read the introduction which describes how to prepare the ready-to-use stencils, and you, too, will be able to add colour and interest to your bedroom and bathroom. Now is the time to start.

America Saint George

BASIC MATERIALS AND TECHNIQUES

Each of the stencils in this book are supplied on special paper in the centre, ready for you to cut out. A variety of paint techniques are used for different surfaces. However, the main technique is stipple stencilling, which is easy and very versatile. By short, quick taps of the stencil brush, walls, furniture, fabric, sisal matting and even glass are decorated, and step-by-step instructions are given opposite and overleaf together with preparation of stencil and basic stencilling techniques. Throughout the book, informative instructions accompany new skills, giving a wide variety of choice.

MATERIALS AND EQUIPMENT

CRAFT KNIFE

This is essential for cutting out your stencils, whether you are using a pull-out from the middle of this book, acetate (mylar) or oiled manilla board (stencil paper). The blade needs to be sharp and clean.

CUTTING MAT

With a good cutting mat beneath your stencil, the cutting out will be made much easier. It will give you a firm and smooth surface on which to lean and will also ensure that you don't cut through onto the work surface by mistake. Preferably use a PVC self-healing cutting mat. These are available in various sizes from any good craft shop.

MASKING TAPE

This is the self-adhesive tape that tears like paper and can be re-used several times before its stick wears out. It is invaluable for stencilling as it can be used when cutting out the stencil, for positioning it on the surface to be stencilled, and also for masking out areas of the design that you might not wish to use (see overleaf).

PAINTS

Modern acrylic paints are excellent. They are inexpensive, versatile and durable, and the range of colours is fabulous. Acrylic paints (see suppliers) are used throughout the book for walls and furniture; fabric paints are used for all fabric and sisal matting. Both of these types of paint are water-soluble. Spray paints are also used as they are the most durable of all stencil paints, allowing for frequent cleaning — perfect for bathrooms. Spray paints need a

solvent like turpentine for cleaning brushes and accidental spillages; the manufacturer's instructions on the can will tell you exactly which solvent is best to use.

To create new colours with acrylic paints, you can easily mix existing shades. Select your paints and mix them together on a tray, stay-wet palette or normal plate. Have a mist water spray to hand in case the paint begins to dry and use cling film (plastic wrap) to cover the paint when it is not in use.

The basic materials needed for stencilling are few — the stencil, paints and brushes.

REPOSITIONABLE SPRAY GLUE

This is a very useful product for sticking a stencil in place before painting through it. It has such a good contact that no paint will slip beneath the edges of the design.

STENCIL BOARDS OR PULL-OUT STENCILS

The stencils produced on this book are on heavy-duty tracing paper which is durable enough for up to ten repeats. To make your own stencils, use either acetate (mylar) or oiled manilla board (stencil paper), available from craft shops. They are easy to use and last for as long as you wish to keep the stencil.

STENCIL BRUSHES

Stencil brushes have short, strong bristles and they should have a little spring in them. Use a different stencil brush for each colour and never wash a brush mid-stencilling as the additional water can cause seepage behind the stencil which will result in destroying your work.

VARNISHES

You might not choose to apply a coat of varnish on top of a stencil, but several coats of polyurethane varnish in either gloss or semi-gloss will protect any stencil that may come up against wear and tear in a bedroom or bathroom. Leave each coat to dry before applying the next.

PREPARING A STENCIL

If you are using one of the stencils from the pull-out section in this book, prepare it as outlined below. If you want to enlarge or reduce any of the featured designs, do this on a photocopier and then transfer the design onto oiled manilla board (stencil paper), available from art shops. To transfer the design, go over the stencil outline on the tracing paper on its reverse side with a very soft pencil. Then position the paper on the manilla board (stencil paper), hold it in place with masking tape, and use the same soft pencil to go over the stencil outline one more time. Remove the tracing paper and neaten the design with your pencil before cutting it out as described in step 2 below.

1 Remove the stencil from the book. The stencils are printed on a thick tracing paper which is perfect for the beginner and advanced stenciller alike. To introduce a base colour for this stencil (see pages 76-9) I made a second base stencil by tracing the outline of the leaf onto tracing paper.

2 Cut out the stencil using a cutting knife and mat, or embroidery scissors. Cut carefully, always changing the position of the stencil to accommodate the cutting line. Keep your support hand away from the blade in case you slip. Cut out the second base stencil on the separate tracing paper.

PAINTING THE STENCIL

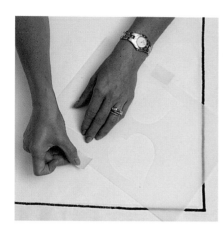

1 Attach the stencil to the surface to be decorated with masking tape or repositionable spray glue on the reverse side of the stencil. Here I am stencilling the background of the design first.

2 Mix your paints to create the colour you first want to use. Here I mixed a little yellow and red to obtain an orange. Massage the paint into the stencil brush bristles and tap it gently onto the palette to ensure the paint is evenly distributed and to remove any excess paint. If the brush is still too soggy, remove the paint by tapping onto a kitchen paper towel. Then tap the brush onto the surface to be decorated. When finished, peel off the stencil to reveal the orange base leaves. Here I am stencilling onto a pillow case and to prevent paint seeping through to the back of the case, I took the precaution of placing plastic between the layers.

3 As this design is a double stencil, I repeated steps 1 and 2 with the second stencil. Make sure the stencils are aligned before working on the second one. If you are using acetate (mylar) or tracing paper this is easy as the materials are transparent. If you are using oiled manilla board (stencil paper), however, cut registration marks in the layers of stencils beforehand. Stencil the leaf veins in a darker contrasting colour to give definition to the finished stencil effect.

4 Peel back the stencil to reveal the finished design. To make a fabric paint stencil washable, dry iron on the reverse side of the fabric to fix the paint into the material.

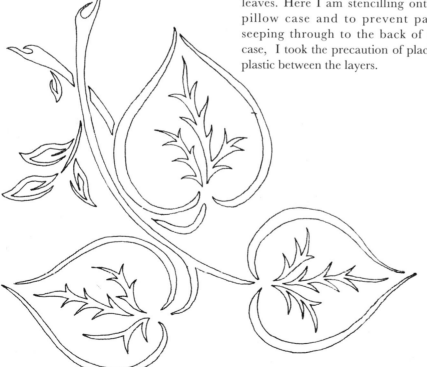

USING MORE COMPLICATED
DOUBLE STENCILS

1 When creating a stencil with several layers, first stencil the part of the design that appears to be on the top. Here I am using the Country Leaves and Flowers stencils that are featured on pages 68-75. Draw the position of the rod design on the wall in pencil and then place the trailing flower stencil over the markings. Stencil the design as described opposite but using acrylics. I used a crimson red with a hint of black.

2 Using pieces of masking tape, fix the rod stencil to the wall in the position marked and you will see the trailing flower showing through. In order not to stencil over these delicate tendrils, cut thin strips of masking tape and curve them over the tendrils, sticking them carefully in place.

3 Stencil the rod. This time I reversed my colours, using mainly black with a hint of red to soften.

4 Peel off the rod stencil together with its masking tape additions to reveal the completed design beneath.

The dramatic rod and its finer accompanying tendrils create a strong country effect.

5 To give the rod a swag and tail effect, I added parts of the trailing flower design at each end. Work one end first and then repeat at the other end, reversing the stencil so that the flowers tumble down the wall in a mirror image. To make the ends of the trailing flowers more tender, only the smaller design elements have been stencilled to mimic nature's growth pattern.

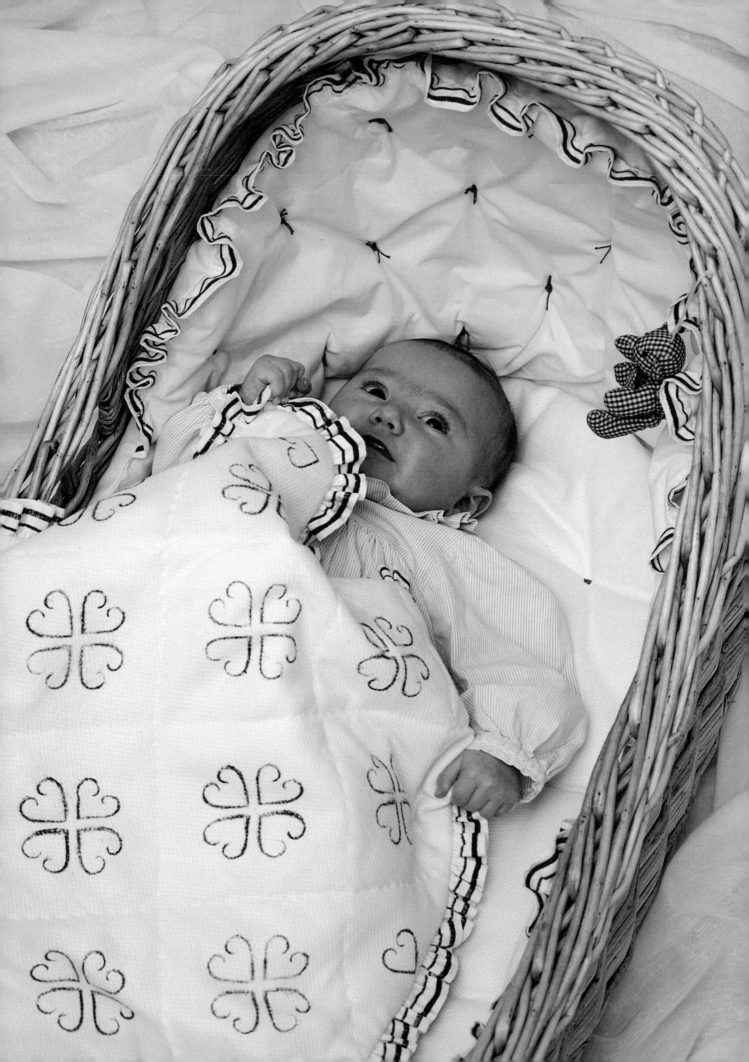

NURSERY HEARTS

It is wonderful to prepare for the birth of a child, whether it is your own baby, a grandchild or that of a friend. A baby is small for such a short time that it is worth enjoying every moment and cosseting the newborn. A wicker baby basket is a lovely feature in the traditional nursery – it is strong, light, transportable and very snug when lined and quilted with stencilled fabric.

When you have gathered together a baby basket from one friend and a high chair from another, a coat of non-toxic paint and some simple stencils will enable you to give a new and coordinated look to your baby's room. To complement the furniture, stencil a frieze of hearts on the wall, or transform plain curtains with a border of hearts.

This charming crib is stencilled with hearts for the new baby. Both the small quilt and little sheet were easy to make and they are fully washable. The lining, mattress, quilt and sheets were made specially for the wicker basket and they avoid draughts, add warmth and make the crib as pretty as possible. Using plain cotton sheeting I lined the crib, adding polyester wadding (batting) for warmth and an edge of striped fuchsia fabric. The quilt was then made from the same material (see below). Using red fabric paint the hearts can be stencilled individually, in rows or double rows as on the sheet, or arranged prettily into a diamond as shown on the quilt. When stencilling a row of hearts, I cut out several hearts together, making it easier to repeat the row along the fabric or wall.

MAKING THE BABY QUILT

YOU WILL NEED

White pique measuring 50 x 70 cm (18 x 25 in)

White cotton sheeting measuring 50 x 70 cm (18 x 25 in)

Polyester wadding (batting) measuring 47 x 67 cm (17 x 24 in)

4.8 m (5 yd) of frill or trim

Heart pull-out stencil (see page 33)

Cutting mat

Masking tape

Fabric paints

Stencil brush

1 Cut out the pique and cotton sheeting for the quilt, and if you are using fabric for the frill, cut this out, too, to twice the length of the outside edge of the quilt.

2 Join together the ends of the frill and then, using the loosest tension on your machine, run two lines of running stitch close to the inside edge. Pull up the frill until it fits neatly around the edge of the quilt.

3 Place the quilt fabrics with right sides together and pin the corners. Sandwich the gathered frill between the materials with the decorated edge of the frill facing into the centre of the quilt, pin and tack (baste). Stitch through all three layers of material leaving a 30 cm (12 in) opening. Stitch together just the frill and the bottom material along the opening.

4 Turn the quilt right sides out. Place the polyester wadding (batting) inside the quilt smoothing out the corners and hand stitch the opening to close.

5 To achieve the diamond quilting, lay a measuring tape across the quilt at regular intervals (my diamonds are 11 x 11 cm [$4^{1}/_{3}$ in x $4^{1}/_{3}$ in]), pin and then tack (baste). I quilted by hand, but machine stitching is also effective.

6 Stencil the hearts using fabric paint into each diamond. In the half diamonds, place a single heart.

BABY'S BATHROOM

With small babies, a great deal of time is spent bathing and changing, so a small area set aside with everything to hand is helpful. Every surface should be selected for their smooth finish to enable easy cleaning. The changing mat used opposite is made from inexpensive foam covered with a tough plastic mat with raised surfaces to prevent a young baby from rolling off. Both a plain mat and wall tiles are perfect to stencil on using spray paint (see below). If, in a few years, the stencils begin to fade, either remove them with nail polish remover and stencil a different motif, or reposition the stencil over the fading one and re-spray.

   The small stencil hearts can be used in various combinations to create different designs. Here, I have used the same design on both the tiles and the nappy (diaper) changer to link them. But consider stencilling rows of smaller hearts on the top and bottom of the tiles or just a single, larger, one in the centre. Vary the position of the heart stencils to suit the size of your tile. If you are stencilling a large area, cut out a stencil with at least two tile repeats

USING SPRAY PAINT

YOU WILL NEED

Heart pull-out stencil (see page 33)

Cutting mat

Masking tape

Craft knife or small embroidery
scissors

Repositionable spray glue

Spray paints

1 Prepare your stencil as described on page 9. Spray the back of the stencil with repositionable glue. This makes the stencil very slightly sticky and it adheres well to the wall avoiding any seepage of spray paint beneath. If you are using the stencil repeatedly, also use masking tape.

Previous page: *White accessories in the nursery are always attractive, especially if they are decorated with bright primary colours such as the blue hearts used here.*

2 It is most important with spray paint to totally surround the stencil area. Use overlapping newspaper firmly stuck into position with masking tape. Then apply the paint, which is very simple as long as you do not spray directly at the stencil. Instead, spray directly at a hand-held paper guard and the force of the paint will make a light mist which settles in the stencil apertures.

3 Remove the newspaper surround and peel back the stencil board to reveal the design beneath. Then position the card ready for further use. The stencilling will vary each time you do it, but do not let this worry you as it adds interest to the design.

SAILING BOATS

These brightly coloured boats have been stencilled so that they look as though they are racing back and forth along the nursery wall. Their bows cut into the sea and the rippling waves follow in the small boats' wake. Little buoys bob among the boats, redirecting them onto an accurate course.

Watching boats closely as they sail into the wind at sea or in a river gives me great pleasure. I love to watch their billowing sails and the gurgle of water as they go about, altering their course, and tacking back and forth. Today, many sails have wonderful colour combinations and it is these that inspired this design for the nursery. It is one that is made especially suitable for babies and young children by its primary colours and on these pages and overleaf you can see that it works very well on all surfaces and accessories in the nursery. Of course, there is no reason why you couldn't also use it in a bathroom.

By tilting the boats and buoys, the continuous movement of the sea is evoked and with these three elements, a story of a might storm, say, or a calm meander along a river, could be told.

Below and opposite I show several different ways of using the stencil whether it be as a frieze, or bed linen, on a laundry bag or on a toy box. Descriptions are given below for re-creating each of these ideas, together with a bedside lamp on page 22. Stencils with small, separate elements, as here, are very versatile, especially colour-wise and you should feel free to exploit them in any way you choose.

Left: *By varying the colour combinations on the sails and boat, and changing the angle of each one, one simple stencil need never look the same.*

Opposite: *The toy box beneath the bed is really an old file storage box painted white and spattered with primary colour paints using a toothbrush. The smaller buoys have been stencilled so that they jauntily tip back and forth among the waves. A coat of clear acrylic varnish both inside and out will prevent the box from discolouring.*

STENCILLING A FRIEZE

Using a very soft pencil, measuring tape and ruler, draw a line along the wall for where you want the frieze to fall. Even though the boats have a lot of movement, it is helpful to use a spirit level if you have one, particularly if the house is older and the floor to frieze measurement unreliable. When drawing the frieze, take into account the proportions of the smaller furniture found in a nursery and the height of a child and position the guide line slightly lower down than you might normally do. If the walls are very high, consider adding small stencilled details, scattering the upper wall and ceiling with stencilled moons and stars, for example. Here I chose to position the frieze just above the cot (crib) side, running past a colourful chest of drawers.

YOU WILL NEED

Soft pencil

Measuring tape

Spirit level

Sailing boats pull-out stencil
(see page 35)

Cutting mat

Masking tape

Craft knife or small embroidery
scissors

Repositionable spray glue (optional)

Acrylic paints

Stencil brushes

1 Prepare your stencil as described on page 9. Then attach it to the wall using masking tape. If, like these boats, you want each sail to be a different colour, place a little masking tape over the adjoining sail. Stencil one sail in one colour; remove the masking tape and when the paint is dry place the tape over the coloured sail and stencil the second sail. Do the same for the boat hull.

2 Stencil one boat, then move along the wall and stencil a buoy and some waves, and then the next boat. Working in this way avoids large gaps in the frieze occurring, or a bottle-neck of boats in one position.

3 To make mirror images and vary the look of the elements, use the other side of the stencil. The waves could also be used upside down for variety.

STENCILLING ONTO BED LINEN AND A LAUNDRY BAG

Stencilling on fabric is most effective and results in the total transformation of an inexpensive piece of cotton. Double over a piece of cotton sheeting, right sides facing, to the dimensions of the child's quilt or pillow and sew around two sides. Then hem the end edges, catching gingham and tartan ties in place to secure the cover or pillow case. Turn the cover right sides out and iron.

Place a sheet of plastic (or a large plastic bag) between the front and back of the cover so that no paint marks the back. Then stencil on the design using fabric paints, moving the plastic bag beneath as you work over the fabric. At the top of the quilt shown opposite, I stencilled stars for even sweeter dreams. To fix the paint, dry iron on the reverse of the fabric to the material's temperature tolerance.

The laundry bag is a remnant from the quilt cover, with the boats storing laundry for the washing machine's hold. Tied with a red gingham ribbon, the laundry bag is a practical addition to a young child's room.

CONTINUING THE THEME

So often, the nursery seems to be the natural place in which to stencil and there are all sorts of different places in which you can continue this boating theme. Beware over doing it, however. Other ideas to consider are stencilling the curtains, the cot (crib) (especially if you have one of those old-fashioned cots (cribs) with solid ends), or that small set of wooden shelves you picked up from the bric à brac store. A quick sand down and lick of paint to tidy it up, and then away you go with the acrylic paints and stencils.

Alternatively, how about stencilling a lampshade, as shown here? Either stencil onto a bought lamp, gently supporting the shade, or transfer the shape of the shade onto lightweight card by gently rolling it across the card, drawing around the shade as you do so. Then stencil onto the card, cut it out, curve the card around the shade and secure it with glue.

TRAILING RIBBONS AND FLOWERS

This little white bedroom was greatly enhanced by gentle and imaginative stencilling. When a room is very small, stencilling can improve the wall surfaces without making the room look cluttered or too busy.

This design of trailing ribbons and flowers was directly influenced by some curtain material that I had. If you have a favourite material with distinctive elements, place tracing paper over them, copy the outlines and then transfer your design onto stencil paper as I did here (see page 9). Use the colours within your material for the stencilling, creating a natural harmony of tones within your room. The added detail of trailing ribbon on the bedside drawers featured overleaf is an element taken from the stencil.

I decided to use this stencil several times around the room as 'hanging panels'. To make this easier I cut out the whole panel, repeating elements of the stencil supplied within this book several times.

To make the stencil for the additional decorative polka dots I have discovered a neat little trick. For years I used to cut them by hand, but if you hunt around for a leather hole puncher, you should get a 4cm (1½ in) cylindrical tube which, with the aid of a hammer, punches polka dots with ease out of oiled manilla board (stencil paper).

A problem which confronted me here was that the walls within this eighteenth-century house had uneven bulges and the cornice was not straight to a spirit level. So which line do you go with to make your stencil look straight on the wall? Often a spirit level is the best guide to position your stencil. Then stand back and very slightly adjust the stencil to sit more comfortably within the room's curves. The ribbons and flowers stencil, with its soft tumbling lines, is ideal for old walls. Never be tempted to use a rigid, geometric stencil on walls like this as the strict lines will only accentuate further the uneven blemishes.

23

USING STENCILS IN PANELS

Stencils can be used in so many different ways. Here I used each corner stencil and reversed it to form a 'hanging panel' design; by varying the repeats, a lively movement is created. The basic stencil is a band of ribbon, a band of ribbon with flowers, and finally a flower stem branching out from the corner. Each of these elements can be used individually or together. Within my formation I have repeated blocks of these designs: one ribbon design across the top and three flower and ribbon designs for the descent, ending with one more plain ribbon design. For the reversed image, a single band of ribbon is used along the top, descending into only two repeats of ribbons and flowers and ending in one ribbon design. This makes the right-hand side of the panel shorter and adds interest. For the paint, I chose two colours, ultramarine blue and cadmium yellow. Mixed together, these give the rather deep leaf green which is used on the curtain. If at all possible, I limit my colours while stencilling and tend instead to use the same colour but with more or less application of paint, lightening or darkening the tone of a single colour.

YOU WILL NEED

Ribbons and flowers pull-out stencil
(see page 37)

Sheet mat acetate (mylar) or
oiled manilla board (stencil paper)

Tracing paper (optional)

Soft pencil

Masking tape

Cutting mat

Craft knife or small embroidery
scissors

Repositionable spray glue (optional)

Acrylic paints

Stencil brushes

1 When repeating a stencil several times I find it easier to cut it out from oiled manilla board (stencil paper) (see page 9). Then fix the stencil to the surface which you are going to paint using the masking tape or repositionable spray glue and stencil with the acrylic paints as described on page 9. Follow the sequence given above to create the panels. In the photograph above I am working on the third panel, stencilling the second repeat of flowers and ribbons.

2 To finish the design with a trailing ribbon turn the whole stencil through 90 degrees, so that it is on its side. Then stencil the ribbon design only, in a descending trail. Stencil as many of the polka dots as you like. Here I faded them out as the stencil design descended.

*Panels of decorative stencilling can completely
transform a plain white room.*

CURTAINS

Translucent white curtains are often necessary in an overlooked bedroom, and incorporating them delicately within the window setting can be a pleasing solution. The design on this curtain fabric is strong and an old favourite from my childhood. The yellow frill picks out the small amount of yellow within the fabric, and so I used yellow for the stencil polka dots on the voile and on the bed linen below.

BED LINEN

The bed linen is top-stitched with yellow and blue. I find it easier to top-stitch a plain white pillow case and sheet rather than try to find a perfect match in a shop. The bedside drawers were first given a soft wash of green with an even softer wash of white over the top. I then stencilled the tumbling ribbon design in blue on either side of the knobs, to give the room a harmonious, light and airy effect.

CAMELLIAS

This wonderfully large and airy bedroom (see the photograph overleaf) has been furnished with silk curtains, bed curtains and bedcover to keep the atmosphere light. They have all been stencilled with a suitably feminine design featuring camellias painted in soft reds, blues and greens.

I must admit that this is my mother's bedroom and she was quite determined to have an elegant, soft feel to the room. Her original idea was to have cherry blossom with a Chinese influence, but after I had cut every last detail, it was vetoed as too fussy. So the exceptional camellias that grace her garden path became the theme.

Two main branches of camellias are featured. The first is a larger one with a main stem and five flowers in varying stages of opening together with a tight bud. The second is a smaller branch made up of two fine branch ends crossing each other. These lighter branches have a combination of two flower heads and two buds. The advantage of finer, separate branches is that they can be separated and used individually. My mother also insisted on a selection of pretty butterflies which were used in abundance.

Blue butterflies flit in and out among the camellia flowers and leaves — spring is forever present in this bedroom.

STENCILLING CURTAINS

There are three options of paint for stencilling onto fabric — fabric paint, spray paint or air brushing with ink. It was this last option that I went for here because of the sheer amount of fabric to be covered (in total 45 metres, or 50 yards!). Inexpensive airbrushes are now available, and stencilling does not require a finer, expensive version. Use the airbrush just as you would car spray paint (see pages 16-17), always in a well-ventilated room. However, the force is not as strong as from a can, so you will have to aim the inks more towards the stencil for a direct hit.

The larger camellias are stencilled near to the hem; the next row is stencilled with the larger camellias mixed with the occasional lighter combination; and then the next row is predominately the smaller camellias. Finally, the last row has only the smaller stencils, completely fading into the top pleating, giving the curtains a natural balance. The curtain ties were stencilled with longer sprigs of camellias that are not too overwhelming.

YOU WILL NEED

Soft pencil

Camellias stencils
(see pages 32, 39 and 41)

Cutting mat

Masking tape

Craft knife or small embroidery scissors

Repositionable spray glue (optional)

Fabric paints

Stencil brushes

Previous page:
The flexibility of these stencils means that the scale and design can be varied according to its context. Here the quilted bedspread features the larger elements of the camellia stencil spread out to give some breathing space. The quilt centre has trailing elements of the smaller stencil made into an oval design by masking off the stems, which could have looked straggly. The bed curtain makes great play of the butterflies. They have been enlarged and stencilled onto voile and the end result is a restful and airy backdrop.

UNIFYING A BEDROOM
AND BATHROOM

By using the same stencil in the adjoining bathroom and on the same fabric, the two rooms lead effortlessly one into the other. The gathered and frilled Austrian blind shown below was the easiest to stencil because there weren't such acres of fabric to deal with as with the bedroom curtains. Covered with only the smaller camellia stencil (see page 39) and flitting butterflies (see page 41) the blind is lovely, cascading in folds over the window. A blind is frequently more practical in a bathroom as it can be hoisted out of the way of splashing water.

CAMELLIAS

This is the larger of the two camellia sprigs featured on pages 27-31. Pull-out stencils for the simpler camellia sprig and the butterflies are given on pages 39 and 41. To transfer this stencil see page 9.

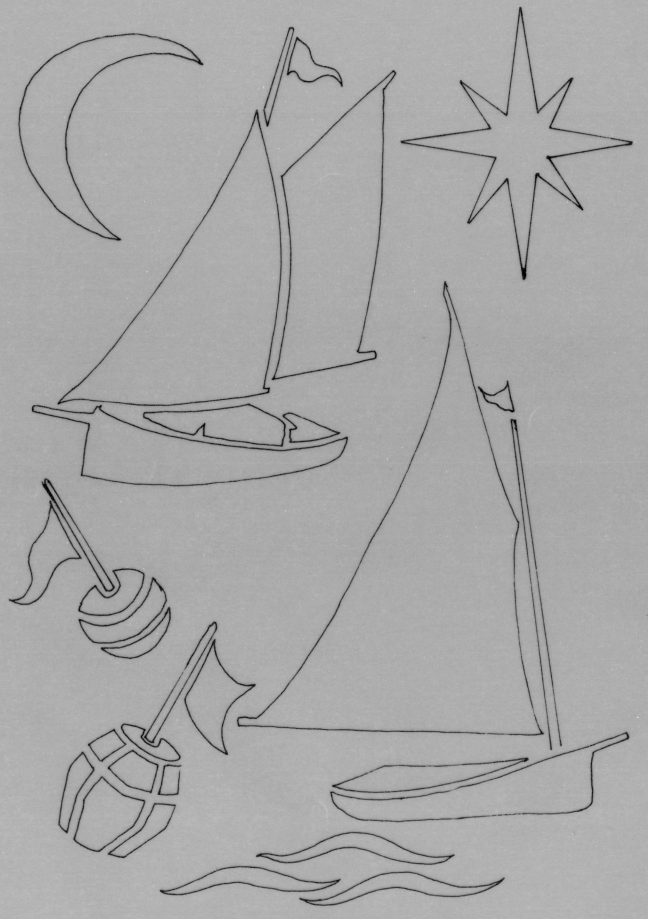

35

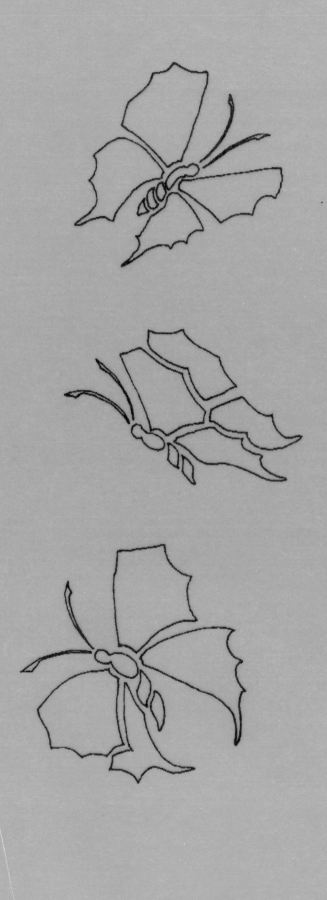

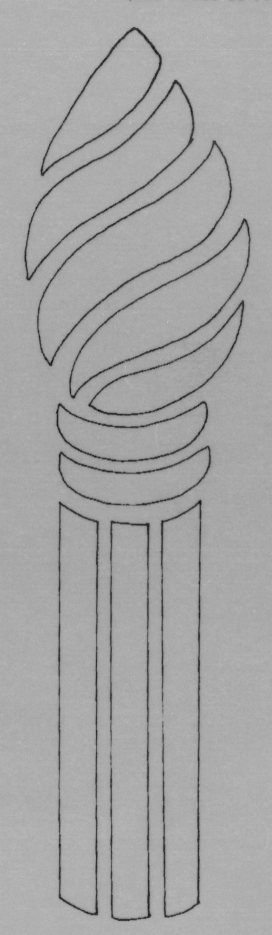

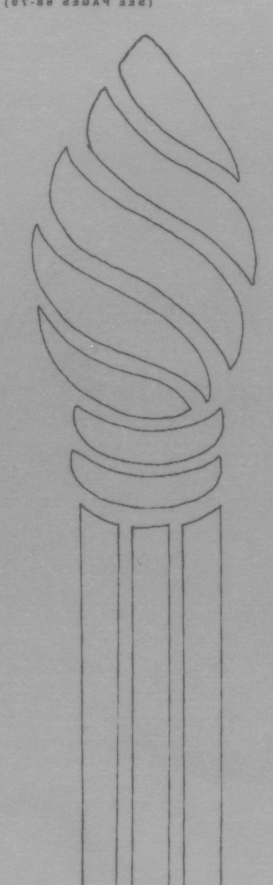

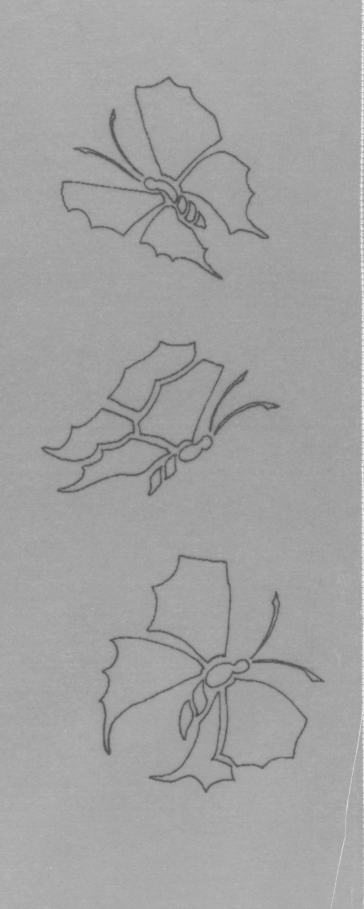

MEDITERRANEAN OLIVES

This design is inspired by the warm mustard, cream and terracotta colours of Provence and features a trail of meandering olives traversing the wall. It brings a little of the holiday environment back home and reflects the natural world.

Whenever I go on holiday I bring back designs in a sketch book or in my head and recreate a feel and mood. This one was inspired by the massive gnarled olive trees of the Mediterranean with twisting branches and rustling leaves. Trudging up a narrow hill path in Provence I noticed lots of villagers who were, I thought, folding large sheets. Then I realized they were shaking the olive trees and the olives were falling into the outstretched sheeting, the boys in the branches laughing with pleasure. So my stencil olives remind me of all these simple delights.

It is wonderful to snuggle into bed surrounded by the sprigs of olive leaves tumbling down a mosquito net (see overleaf). The curved stencil can be made into a wreath or it can undulate back and forth in a frieze across the wall, around the edges of a rug or over a wooden floor.

Smaller parts of the olives and leaves can be used individually as sprigs on pillows, curtains, covers or as a scattered wall decoration. Stencilled onto card, the scattered olives would make perfect stationery for a guest room drawer.

Enlarging the design on a photocopier (see page 9), gave me a larger scale of stencil which suited the room's proportions better. I painted the lower half of the wall a warm mustard yellow and the top half a deep cream, then spattered a cocktail of colours – terracotta, olive green and flecks of purple – over the wall. I did this by coating a scrubbing brush with paint, holding it in front of the wall and then rubbing my rubber-gloved hand over the whole surface so that flecks and spatters coloured the wall. Some flecks were rather large, so I massaged them into the wall, creating a swirling effect.

STENCILLING ON WALLS WITH ACRYLIC PAINT

YOU WILL NEED

Mediterranean olives pull-out stencil
(see page 45)

Cutting mat

Masking tape

Craft knife or small embroidery
scissors

Repositionable spray glue (optional)

Acrylic paints

Stencil brushes

1 Place the stencil over the line where the colours join on the wall. In order to make this easier I drew a central line across the middle of the stencil and simply positioned it over the line on the wall each time.

2 Reuse the same olive green and purple shades, and colour the leaves olive green and the olives purple. I also added hints of purple to the leaves, the additional tone giving them a subtle shading and an accentuated sense of movement.

The olive stencil could also climb up and down the walls as a repeating design. The colours chosen for the stencil are those used in the spattering of the paint to soften and age the wall surface. By using a few of the same colours you will achieve a natural harmony within your work.

Spattering the surface of the wall creates an interesting background for the stencilling and links together the colours of the design.

Opposite: This stencil design brings the warm, earthy tones of Provence into the bedroom.

A stencilled mosquito net and pillows evoke memories of warm summer nights and the delicious scent of trees and flowers wafting through open windows.

STENCILLED LINEN

Stencilling on bedroom linen is most effective and fully washable when fabric paints are used. To fix fabric paints before washing, simply iron the stencil on the reverse side for a few minutes at the fabric's temperature tolerance.

Here I isolated the individual olive sprigs from the main stencil and stencilled them, dancing around the square pillow case with the olives facing the pillow edge. The long bolster pillow has the olives stencilled around the tied cuff. Scattered over the mosquito net are tumbling olives (see also page 50), as if they were dropping, ripe from the tree. The olives hang suspended in mid-air, never to reach the ground. As the mosquito net tumbles over the white linen sheets, the olives leave a delightfully delicate shadow design. Although the mosquito net is 100 per cent nylon, which normally does not absorb fabric paint, these fibres are soft enough that stencilling on the netting has proved most successful. Hopefully these delicious olives will not attract the mosquitos.

The Mediterranean olives stencil is very versatile. Use it vertically,
horizontally, winding around corners or just as a simple spray, as here.
A pull-out stencil is provided on page 45.

OLIVE BATHROOM

The delicate, gently undulating, olive branch used in the bedroom on pages 49-53 also trails around this small bathroom, meandering up and down at dado rail height. The branches double back and turn corners with ease. They are also reversed in places so that the stencil will accommodate any shape that is required of it.

As shown in the photograph below, the olive stencil flows neatly around the corner of the ceramic tiles, softening the acute tile edge. In this way it also means that the design can continue to circle the bathroom.

Stencilling around corners or into corners can be difficult. The best method is to fold the stencil paper, fitting it snugly into the corner. Attach it with additional masking tape to retain the folded position and stencil; allow for a gentler application of paint on the 90-degree fold to avoid the risk of potential seepage of paint behind the stencil onto the wall. On completion, flatten the stencil once more, pressing out the crease by drawing your thumb firmly down the line.

If you are stencilling over a corner that juts out, it is easier to position the stencil firmly with masking tape and stencil one side of the wall. Then carefully place the continuation of the stencil on the next wall face, ensuring the design is well aligned.

A light, semi-translucent Indian cotton curtain (see opposite and overleaf) gives privacy in the bathroom. The full stencil trail of the Mediterranean olives meanders around the curtain edge, beginning beneath the curtain heading, descending into the sweeping curve, following the curtain hem and then finally up the last side. Small sprigs of olive details taken from the main stencil fill the rest of the curtain, tumbling over the translucent billowing cotton.

Opposite: *The Mediterranean olives stencil is very flexible as it has been designed to work well in both straight lines and around corners, as shown on these soft cotton curtains.*

Left: *An area of ceramic tiles can be softened by curving a stencil design around the edge. The fluidity of the Mediterranean olives are especially successful as they meander across the wall.*

Overleaf: *By stencilling the same design onto hand-towels and furniture as well as walls and soft furnishings, a room can be quickly and attractively coordinated.*

STENCILLING ON GLASS

The addition of this coordinating curtain adds harmony to the room. Depending on how overlooked your bathroom is, and which pattern you choose, stencilling onto the glass can be most effective not only for privacy but also adding decorative interest. To stencil glass, either use translucent glass paint which can be bought from a specialist art shop, or car spray paint, which is equally durable.

Both glass paints and car spray paints can be used to give a mock stained-glass window or, if nature is too far away, stencil leaves lingering over the window as they might in a cottage in the country. Stencilled glass can be a safety measure; I most recently stencilled large patio sheet glass doors with butterflies apparently flittering in the air to warn any visitors of the sheet glass doors.

YOU WILL NEED

Mediterranean olives pull-out stencil (see page 45)

Cutting mat

Masking tape

Craft knife or small embroidery scissors

Repositionable spray glue

Translucent glass paints

White spirit (mineral spirit)

Stencil brushes

1 Prepare the pull-out stencil as described on page 9. If you are only using a section of the stencil, use masking tape to cover those areas that you don't wish to paint through (see page 11).

2 Fix the stencil to the window with masking tape and then apply the glass paint using the stippling method outlined on page 10. The glass paint is soluble with white spirit and can be diluted to give softer, shadow effects.

COORDINATING A BATHROOM

The two ideas shown on this page are but a sample of what you might decide to decorate in your bathroom to give it a strong sense of coordination. So consider stencilling around the door's architrave, on the edge of the bath if the surround is made of wood, sprigs on plain white tiles, or adding a spray or two to a lampshade. One word of warning, though — don't go overboard with this technique. As simple as stencilling might be to apply, there is a fine line between the room looking quite wonderful or just downright overdone.

Another trick when planning your stencilling is to change the scale of the stencil, or perhaps just a detail or two of it. Instructions for re-scaling a design are given on page 9. In this bathroom, for example, the surround of the curtain could have been stencilled with larger sprigs running around the edge in an ordered manner, in place of the existing complete stencil. The centre of the fabric could then have been decorated with a wreath made by taking small elements of the main stencil and curving it around on itself.

Fabric paints are just as easy to apply as acrylics are to walls, and here I have stencilled details from the Mediterranean olives stencil onto a simple cotton hand towel and also onto a pair of lightweight summer pyjamas. By limiting the stencil to a single olive on the pyjama bottoms, the end result is understated and most attractive.

Additional stencil sprigs of olives are reversed and tilted so that they dance along a soft border weave on the towels. Summer pyjamas have also been stencilled, completing the soft Mediterranean effect.

BRIGHTLY
GEOMETRICAL

Bright fabric cushions were chosen to double as pillows at night-time and also to coordinate with the fabric throw on the opened bed. The simple stencil design is used differently on each cushion, resulting in a varied, yet still coordinated, look.

MAKING A REPEAT PATTERN

YOU WILL NEED

Geometric pull-out stencil
(see page 47)

Cutting mat

Masking tape

Craft knife or small embroidery scissors

Repositionable spray glue

Acrylic paints

Stencil brushes

1 Prepare your pull-out stencil from page 47 as described on page 9 and attach it to the wall using either repositionable spray glue or masking tape. Follow a pencilled line for the stencil positioning (see page 20).

2 Place a small amount of acrylic paint onto a plate and, using a stencil brush, stipple onto the wall as described on page 10.

3 Remove the stencil and place it slightly over the painted stencil so that the repeat pattern continuation is uninterrupted. The stencil is also used vertically on the paper bag lampshade.

Sofa beds are both practical and economical either for a studio room or as an occasional bed within a larger house. One of the problems of living in a studio room, however, is the lack of space and the way to overcome this is by making every item that you buy serve two purposes. In this particular room, the sofa during the day can transform into a bed at night; the larger sofa cushions become the night-time pillows, and the stacking linen-covered boxes are ideal for clothes storage and double as bedside or coffee tables. To give a small room the illusion of greater space, the walls were painted white and the stencilled frieze adds detail and interest.

The stencil design featured on the cushions and on the wall is both economical and versatile. The basic outline has a wrought iron feel to it and when it is used in different sizes, and with or without its tendrils, the heart-like shape combines in any manner of patterns.

Stencilled just between the sofa back and large poster, the frieze has a long straight run that accentuates the length of the wall to the maximum effect.

When the sofa bed is opened up (see overleaf), more stencilling is revealed both as a continual vertical border on the sheet cuff, over-stitched with black, and on the fitted bottom sheet with the stencil design scattered over it. Both are very effective, contributing to the subtle coordination of the room. The whole is just perfect for a lengthy weekend breakfast with the newspapers or when you are hastily rising to the alarm during the week.

Opposite and overleaf: A sofa by day, the versatile piece of furniture becomes a bed by night. The stencilled theme has been continued onto the bed linen so that the room looks good whether it is a sitting room or bedroom.

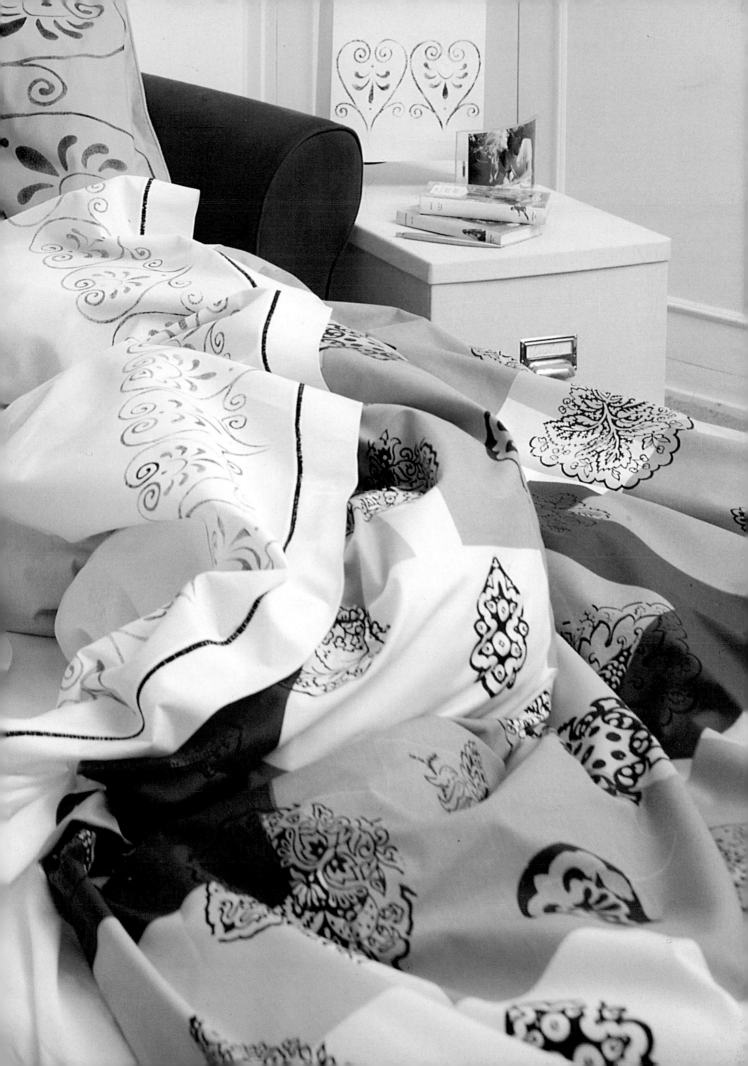

PLANNING A GEOMETRIC PATTERN

To establish the central lines, fold your cushion cover into quarters and pin on the folds. When unfolded, the pins mark the central lines from which each stencil position is measured. Experiment with the design on rough paper, trying it in different combinations and sizes. When you are happy with your work, mark the centre of each quarter of the cushion and position your stencil in the appropriate place.

On the pink cushion shown below, the design is used horizontally and as a mirror image from the central lines. At the corners, the inside scroll work would have overlapped, so it was masked off with tape to make a neat corner

detail. The uniform black looks smart and crisp both on the coloured cushions and white walls, lamp, and sheets.

For the blue and yellow cushions, the stencil design was greatly enlarged using a photocopier. The enlarged design was then individually stencilled into each quarter; but on the blue cushion, the scroll design was masked out with tape. On the yellow cushion, only one pair of the diagonals feature the scroll which would otherwise have overlapped each other and looked very messy. Vary your designs, repeats and positioning as much as possible. This adds a subtle degree of interest to a room.

BLACK AND WHITE GEOMETRIC BATHROOM

If you have an en suite bathroom or it is near to your bedroom, you may want to use the stencil theme in both rooms. With some amending, the design can remain essentially the same and yet a little different. For the bathroom featured overleaf, I chose to add simple straight lines to resemble moulding.

It is always fun adapting a design and masking tape is, of course, invaluable for this. Blocking out areas is perhaps the simplest way of changing a look or just using a small part. But you can also, as here, add to a design, perhaps taking an element from another stencil you like to use, or creating something totally new. For this particular bathroom, I felt it was right to adhere to the simplicity of the basic stencil. As ceramic tiles are used so frequently in a bathroom, and there are many styles of ceramic mouldings available, I thought it would be especially suitable to play on this theme. By cutting the parallel strips so that the spaces between each are not directly over each other, the whole has a sense of movement. The lines could also be run beneath the design if you required more definition.

I chose to stencil the 'moulding' in black to retain the modern simplicity of black on white. However, red would have worked just as well, adding some more colour to the colour scheme. The red stitching in the bath mat and the red soap and other washing accessories would have tied in extremely well with this idea.

If you have an en suite bathroom or it is near to your bedroom, you may want to use the stencil theme in both rooms. With some amending, the design can remain essentially the same and yet a little different. For the bathroom featured overleaf, I chose to add simple straight lines to resemble moulding.

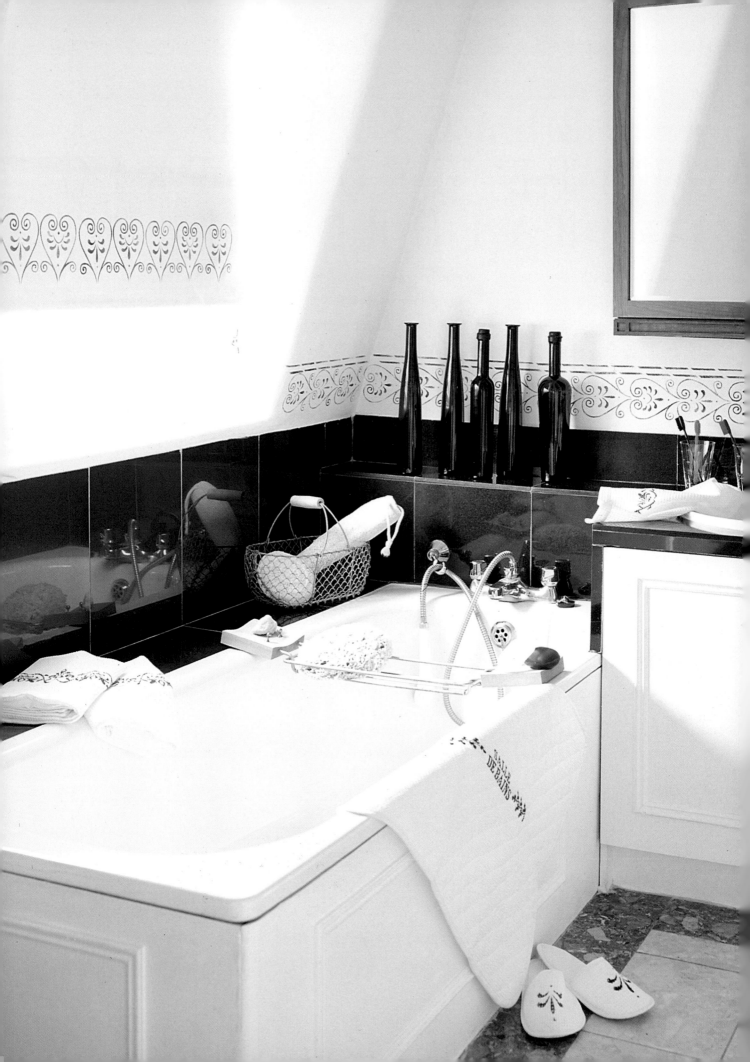

MAKING A SMALL SPACE LOOK LARGER

As this bathroom is quite small, is has been enhanced by running a continuous stencil frieze around the room. The geometry of the design successfully leads the eye around the wall. The blind has been stencilled using fabric paint and with the design used vertically. For easy positioning, I started in the middle of the blind and worked outwards. Always remove any window furnishings from the window as the danger of just slipping through the glass is too great a risk to take. As an additional touch, the smallest element of the stencil design has been placed on the slippers!

YOU WILL NEED

Geometric pull-out stencil
(see page 47)

Cutting mat

Masking tape

Craft knife or small embroidery
scissors

Repositionable spray glue

Acrylic and fabric paints

Stencil brushes

1 Prepare your pull-out stencil as described on page 9. Plan your design on rough paper. Here the basic design is running in the same direction, but you might decide to stencil them in symmetrical pairs, as on the cushion on page 62.

2 Fasten the stencil to the wall or blind using repositionable spray glue or masking tape and apply the paint with a stencil brush as described on page 10.

3 If you have used fabric paints, iron the fabric on the reverse side at the highest temperature that the material can tolerate to fix the design in place.

Such a simple piece of stencilling, and yet what fun to tie-in your slippers with the bathroom and bedroom decor!

Opposite: *A light and airy bathroom remains that way with a small stencil that has been applied using just one colour of paint.*

COUNTRY LEAVES
AND FLOWERS

Moving up into the attic and therefore creating more space, makes room for a new bedroom and bathroom, with a sloping gable roof and skylight windows. A coat of matt emulsion in a deep shade of terracotta was then applied to the walls, ceiling, descending eaves, and the free-standing bedside table (see overleaf). The end result is a room of immense warmth.

The fabric chosen for the bedspread became the inspiration to decorate the bedroom. The fabric design is created from wooden blocks and so a stencil design relates easily to it as stencilling uses the same cutting and spacing principles. The simplest way to design a stencil from your fabric is to directly trace over the material and use elements of the design that have good clear lines that are easy to follow. You will find that some areas will be simpler to translate into a stencil than others. For example, where normally flowers join the stalk and petals, in a stencil these elements are separated from each other by leaving bridges on the stencil board.

Areas can be enlarged or colours changed to form a link between the brought fabric and your stencil design. My stencils are made from two different elements. The first is the delicate flower outline stencil with trailing tendrils featured on the pillow case opposite and above the windows overleaf. This stencil outline is given on pages 74-5; to transfer it to acetate (mylar) or oiled manilla board (stencil paper), see the instructions on pages 9 and 11. The second stencil is the more solid outline of three leaves with veins which are used on the pillow cases on pages 72-3, and also featured in the bathroom on pages 76-9. This particular stencil has also been adapted opposite for use on the lampshade. The design appears in the ready-to-use pull-out section on page 43.

Opposite: *The two stencil designs used in this bedroom complement each other perfectly as one is delicate and flowing, while the other — used on the lampshade — is less ethereal.*

Overleaf: *The flower spray used on the pillow case has also been adapted and stencilled around the tops of the windows. The ridge rod stencil support the natural trailing flowers. Without this, the stencil would appear to be floating rather aimlessly in the air.*

Black Sparrow Press

STENCILLING ON FABRIC

Elements of the two stencil designs used elsewhere in this bedroom have been used especially successfully on the cotton pillow cases. The leaf design has been stencilled diagonally across a corner and the trailing spray of flowers twirl across the black over-stitching to soften the solid line. The stencils have been placed differently on each pillow, enhancing the movement. The smallest element of a tendril has also been reversed and stencilled onto the napkin shown in the photograph opposite forming an abstract design.

You might choose to stencil onto the sheets, too. The curling tendrils would work well running along the top of a sheet to be viewed when it is folded back over the quilt, adding to the tranquillity of this room. Alteratively, the leaves from the other stencil might be usefully employed in a more regular fashion running along the top edge in the same way, but rather like the geometric stencil running along the bathroom wall on page 66. Alternatively — or even in addition? — scatter leaves across the bottom sheet in memory of the end of each year.

Details for stencilling the leaf design are given on page 10 and also featured in the bathroom on pages 76-9. To stencil the spray of flowers, work as shown below.

YOU WILL NEED

Flower spray stencil (see pages 74-5)

Sheet mat acetate (mylar) or oiled manilla board (stencil paper)

Tracing paper (optional)

Waterproof marker (optional)

Cutting mat

Masking tape

Craft knife or small embroidery scissors

Repositionable spray glue

Fabric paints

Stencil brushes

1 Trace the stencil from pages 74-5 and transfer to oiled manilla board (stencil paper) as described on page 9. If you are using acetate (mylar) you can, of course, transfer the design directly onto this using a waterproof marker.

2 Lay the pillow case flat with a plastic sheet placed between the layers of fabric to prevent the paint seeping through to the back of the pillow case. Fasten the stencil in place with masking tape.

3 Apply fabric paints with a stencil brush as described on page 10. Remove the stencil and when the paints are dry, iron on the reverse side of the fabric with the hottest temperature the material can tolerate to fix the paints.

This pretty design is created by using two stencils. The pole and finial appear in the pull-out section on page 41. To reproduce this design you will need to transfer the tendrils to acetate (mylar) or manilla board (stencil paper) as described on page 9. Stencilling this design is featured on page 11.

LEAFY BATHROOM

The stencil in this bathroom is also featured in the bedroom on pages 68-75. It was adapted from the quilt cover and its simplicity makes it perfect for a small bathroom decorated in neutral shades. The bright orange leaves give the room a lift and add a little something in a subtle way.

I experimented by stencilling two different materials: a water-repellent polyester shower curtain and a sisal mat. The mat was just as absorbent as blotting paper and so I over-zealously loaded my brush to begin with, only to discover that this wasn't really necessary. I should really have had a little practice on the reverse side first. However, I then used much less paint on the subsequent leaves and fortunately the variety of tones looked interesting. To fix the paint, spread the sisal mat on the floor and dry-iron it on the top side with a medium heat for three minutes; it is a most efficient mat, perfect for the bathroom.

The stencil is a double stencil. While this may sound complicated, it, in fact, makes sense to work in this way as the background orange can be applied first, safe in the knowledge that the outline will be the perfect shape for the more detailed stencilling that is applied on top. Detailed instructions for using this stencil are given on page 10 and the pull-out stencil can be found in the centre of the book on page 43.

I used fabric paint on the sisal mat and now that I have discovered just how easy it is to work on this surface, will no doubt go on to stencil on other similar natural floorings. Whatever the flooring in your bathroom, whether it is bare floorboards, cork matting or a vinyl, say, this design will work well stencilled onto it. Don't restrict yourself to the colours used here, either. It is far more important that you work with colours that sympathize with your existing decor — unless, of course, you are planning to redecorate your bathroom, or are starting from scratch. These leaves would look equally good in shades of green for that bright spring feeling, or redder tones than the orange and brown used here.

Using the glass painting technique described on page 58, you might also like to consider adding the leaves to the corner of your bathroom mirror or on the window. And if you keep a glass in the bathroom, how about reducing the design on a photocopier and stencilling it on here, too?

The orange towels and bath mat tone in perfectly with the stencils used on the shower curtain and sisal flooring.

STENCILLING ON POLYESTER

Before stencilling on the polyester curtain, I was afraid that what was water-repellent, might also prove to be paint-repellent. Fortunately, it was not the case and I quickly found it was easy to stencil using fabric paint once again. I gradually built-up the stencilling and the finished effect was excellent. As with the sisal mat, I then ironed the shower curtain on its reverse to ensure the stencilling will remain permanent.

YOU WILL NEED

Leaf pull-out stencil
(see page 43)

Tracing paper

Cutting mat

Masking tape

Craft knife or small embroidery
scissors

Repositionable spray glue

Fabric paints

Stencil brushes

1 Remove and prepare the pull-out stencil as described on page 9. Don't forget that this is a double stencil so you will need to prepare the main outline yourself. This is described on page 10.

2 Lay the shower curtain flat and fasten the stencils in place one by one with masking tape or repositionable spray glue.

3 Apply fabric paints with a stencil brush as described on page 10. Work on the main outline first and then stencil the finer details on top. Remove the stencils and when the paints are dry, iron on the reverse side of the fabric. As this fabric is polyester, iron using a low dry heat for a longer period than usual to fix the paints.

SUPPLIERS AND ACKNOWLEDGEMENTS

Daler Rowney fine Art and Graphics Material
Daler Rowney House, Bracknell, Berkshire RG12 8ST
Telephone: 01344 424621
Fax: 01344 486511

Working with these exceptionally high-quality products always gives the best results. The Robert Simmonds stencil brushes come in all sizes, are hard wearing and subtle; System 3 acrylic paint is ideal for most stencilling work, and the screen printing paint is great for fabric. A full 128-page catalogue demonstrates the diversity of all the products, and gives constructive uses for materials.

DMC Creative World
62 Pullman Road, Wigston, Leicester LE18 2DY
Telephone: 0116 2811040
Fax: 0116 2813592

More than 428 colours to choose from in pearl, stranded and sewing cottons, there are also wonderful Zweigart linens, counted weaves and textures. All products are fully washable. There is a comprehensive catalogue and exceptional colour sample charts available from DMC stockists.

Souleiado Provençal Fabrics
78 Rue de Seine, Paris 75006 France
Telephone: 33 01 43 54 15 13
Fax: 33 01 43 54 84 45

There are also many other shops in France and capital cities around the world featuring exquisite collections of Provençal fabrics, both traditional and contemporary designs, in all weights of material. The Souleiado shops are a feast of fabrics not to be missed. My utmost thanks to Souleiado for their exceptional fabric used in Brightly Geometrical on pages 60-4, and also on pages 68-73 where the stencil picks out elements of a Souleiado design.

A particular thank you to both Katherine and Oshi Turner for allowing three-month-old Rufus Alexander Octavian to be photographed; he was a delight!